AUTOMOBILES

AUTOMOBILES

BY JEANNE BENDICK

DISCARD

4/85 WLS 8⁹⁰

J
629.2
B

HIRAM HALLE MEMORIAL LIBRARY
271 Westchester Avenue
Pound Ridge, New York
10576-1714

FRANKLIN WATTS • 1984
NEW YORK • LONDON • TORONTO • SYDNEY
A FIRST BOOK • REVISED EDITION

47942

Illustrations courtesy of Jeanne Bendick

Photographs courtesy of:
Dodge Public Relations: p. 4 (top and bottom);
General Motors: pp. 5 (top), 46 (top and bottom), 55 (bottom), 58;
Chrysler/Plymouth Public Relations: p. 5 (bottom);
Bendick Associates: pp. 8 (top and bottom), 45, 53;
Chevrolet Public Relations: pp. 13, 55 (top);
Buick Public Relations: p. 42.

Library of Congress Cataloging in Publication Data

Bendick, Jeanne.
Automobiles.

(A First book)
Rev. ed. of: The first book of automobiles.
4th ed. 1978.
Includes index.
Summary: Discusses different kinds of cars
and trucks, how they are designed and built,
how they operate, and their varied uses.
1. Automobiles—Juvenile literature.
[1. Automobiles]   I. Bendick, Jeanne.
First book of automobiles.   4th ed. II. Title.
TL147.B4 1984   629.2′2   84-7416
ISBN 0-531-04821-7

Copyright © 1984 by Jeanne Bendick
All rights reserved
Printed in the United States of America
5   4   3   2   1

CONTENTS

(1)
CARS, CARS, CARS!

It would be hard for most of us to imagine living without automobiles.

Automobiles carry millions of people millions of miles a day—to work, to school, on errands and on vacations. Trucks are automobiles that carry products from farms and factories to stores and supermarkets, to other factories and to people's houses. Tank trucks and tow trucks, dump trucks and pickups are automobiles too.

Fire engines are automobiles. So are taxis and buses, vans, jeeps, ambulances, campers, and mobile television studios.

Streets in towns and cities are jammed with cars. Cars cross deserts, climb mountains, and slog through jungles. Some even go through water. All over the world, there are more than four billion automobiles doing their jobs. If they were all driving in line, they would form two lanes in each direction, reaching to the moon and back.

An automobile isn't like a wagon, which needs horses or oxen to pull it. It isn't like a railroad car, which needs a locomotive. An automobile moves by itself. In fact, the word *automobile* means "self-moving." All of its power comes from itself. It doesn't have to be pushed or pulled unless its power is out of order.

FAMILY CARS

Most of the family cars on the road are **standard production cars.** They are general-purpose cars, built in factories. With more than 300 different models, there are lots of choices, depending on what people want their cars to do.

Sedans

Many family cars are sedans. A sedan has front and back seats and holds four, five, or six people. Bigger sedans, called limousines, can seat seven. Some sedans have four doors and some have two. A sedan usually has a trunk for carrying packages, baggage, a spare tire, and other things.

There are also hatchback sedans which have three or five doors, counting the hatchback door. Hatchbacks have an open storage area behind the rear seat, that acts as a trunk.

Whether a car is big or small, it usually has a way to carry the extra things that won't fit inside. Many cars have luggage racks on top. Special racks carry skis, bikes, and canoes. And cars pull trailers with boats, snowmobiles, hot rods, and horses.

Convertibles

Some family cars are convertibles. They have a top that folds back so people can ride in the sun and air. Some cars have sun roofs that slide back to open the top. Some sun roofs are glass, so they let the sun in even if they are closed.

Sports Cars

If there are only two people in the family, or if the family has two cars, they might have a sports car. A sports car usually has two **bucket seats**, with maybe a very small seat behind.

Sports cars are low. The closer to the ground a car is, the faster it can go safely and the easier it is to steer around curves. Most sports cars have a **stick shift** between the seats. The stick is connected to the **transmission** and lets the driver shift the **gears** by hand. (See pages 19–22.) This gives the driver more control in changing the speed of the car and the amount of power to the wheels. Many family sedans have stick shifts, too, but most have automatic transmissions, which change gears automatically.

Sports cars are sometimes convertible. Sometimes they also have a hard top that can be used in the winter. If a sports car has a rack for carrying extra stuff, usually it is fastened to the trunk.

Station Wagons

People who want more room inside the car than a sedan has might have a station wagon. A station wagon can seat six or more passengers and it also has plenty of room for carrying a big load inside, on the deck behind the rear seats. If more room is needed for carrying things, the rear seats fold down to make the deck even bigger. Station wagons also have a door at the back that makes it easier to load and unload big objects.

Mini-Vans

A family that wants even more room might have a mini-van—a cross between a big station wagon and a small bus. Seven to nine people can ride in a mini-van and there will still be room for pets, groceries, baggage, and other things.

A mini-van is usually higher off the ground than a station wagon or a sedan. It may have a big sliding door as well as the regular doors.

Above: *two versions of a four-door sedan.*
Opposite (top): *a convertible with the top
folded back;* (bottom): *this station wagon
seats seven. It has three types of doors:
side hinge, top hinge, and sliding.*

Vans

Full-size vans are much bigger than station wagons. They were first used as delivery trucks and had no windows in the back. Now they come with windows all around and enough seats to carry ten or eleven people. Their square shape makes them look like big bread boxes on wheels.

Some vans have bubble roofs—extra-tall tops that allow people to move around inside without stooping. The bubble roof might fold down when the van is on the road to make it more streamlined.

Some people **customize** their vans. They fix them up with big, soft chairs, curtains, refrigerators and even TVs.

Fixing up vans is a popular hobby. Outside, they may have bubble windows, fancy paint, and all kinds of pictures and decorations. Inside, they can be fixed up like palaces or ranch houses or a scene from the owner's favorite story.

"Vanners" have competitions, and prizes are given for the most beautiful vans. Some vans are so fancy and expensive that they are never driven. They are loaded onto bigger trucks and carried to van shows.

RECREATIONAL VEHICLES

A lot of people have vans that are really mini-homes on wheels. They travel in them, camp, explore, and use them just for fun. They are called **RVs**, which is short for "recreational vehicles"—vehicles used for fun.

The first RV vans were secondhand commercial vans, fixed up by surfers to carry their surfboards to the beach and to use as shelter from the sun and wind. Commercial vans aren't allowed on some parkways, so small windows were put into the sides to make the vans into RVs, which are allowed.

Other kinds of sports people began fixing up vans to carry their own kinds of equipment—motorcycles, dune buggies, canoes, outboard motors, skis, hunting and fishing gear. Some people put in a place to sleep and cooking equipment and maybe a refrigerator and a TV. Now you can buy vans with all this and more.

Some RVs can sleep up to eight people. Families use them for vacations in the mountains or at the beach or anywhere else they want to go. They are moving hotels. You can buy RVs with all the comforts of home—a kitchen and bathroom, a place to sleep, eat, and sit and watch the scenery go by.

PICKUPS

People who live in the country, on farms or ranches, often use a pickup truck as the family car. A pickup has a **cab** in front, for people to ride in. (*Cab* is short for *cabin*.) The back is open for carrying supplies.

More and more, though, people who live in suburbs, towns, and cities are driving pickups, too, just because they like the way they look. These pickups are not really work cars. They have power steering and power windows, air conditioning, stereos, and even sun roofs.

Many families with pickups have campers that fit right over the back of the truck, which is called the *bed*. So pickups can also be used for trips and vacations.

Top: *a pickup truck with a camper attached to the bed.* Bottom: *many mobile homes are located in mobile-home parks.*

CAMPERS AND
MOTOR HOMES

A camper can be a pickup truck with a box mounted on the bed to hold beds and camping equipment. It can be a mini-van or van with simple living equipment built in. Small campers may have only beds, a small cooking stove, and a refrigerator. Larger campers are sometimes motor homes and can be as completely equipped as a house, with a living room, bedroom, dining area, bath and kitchen, air conditioning, phone, and TV.

Many families have a camper trailer instead of an RV. The main difference is that the camper must be pulled by a car or truck because it doesn't have its own motor. You are not supposed to ride in a camper trailer when it is on the road.

Once people could park their campers off by themselves, under the trees somewhere in a national forest or at the seashore. Now there are so many people who enjoy camping in their RVs and campers that the places where they park are like small cities.

There are markets and other services at these camper parks. You can connect your camper into the park's electricity, telephone line, and water and sewage systems. Campers are lined up in rows, and rent is paid for the space. Some RVers even put out awnings and porch furniture.

MOBILE HOMES

"Mobile homes" sound as if they move from place to place, but really they aren't very mobile. A mobile home is big and it usually has several rooms. The difference between a mobile home and a small, regular house is that a mobile home comes with wheels and can be moved by a large truck. The only time most people move a mobile home is when they bring it from the factory to their lot, usually in a mobile home park.

Some mobile home parks look like big parking lots with rows of mobile homes. Others have trees, yards, gardens, and swimming pools. Often the wheels are removed and the mobile home is set right into the ground like an ordinary house.

Mobile homes are moved by the same kind of big truck tractors that pull all kinds of commercial loads along the highways. Because mobile homes are so big, the whole load moves very slowly. Usually they carry signs saying: OVERSIZED LOAD. Sometimes a car drives in front of the load, with another behind, to warn other drivers.

OFF-ROAD VEHICLES

Some cars are specially made for rough, hard driving in sand or snow or mud and even where there are no roads. They usually have more space between the bottom of the car and the ground than ordinary cars have. They have heavier bodies, stiffer springs, and some extra low gears which can give more power when it is needed. (See page 23.)

These vehicles have **four-wheel drive**. Family cars often have power in only one set of wheels—the front or the rear wheels. A car with four-wheel drive has **drive shafts** to both the front and rear wheels. This gives the front wheels power to pull the car through rough places while the rear wheels push it. The driver can select two-wheel or four-wheel drive. Two-wheel drive is used on smooth roads where extra power is not needed. Four-wheel drive is good in deep snow or mud and across rough country. But it is slower and harder on the car and uses much more gas.

The army jeeps that were first used in World War II had four-wheel drive and for a long time most four-wheel-drive vehicles looked like jeeps or trucks. Now, it is hard to tell a four-wheel-drive vehicle from any other kind. Many cars, station wagons, and pickups come with four-wheel drive.

There are new four-wheel drive cars that are not off-road, but use their four-wheel drive for everyday driving, on snowy or slippery roads or on gravel. Probably, all future standard production cars will have four-wheel drive before long.

All Terrain Vehicles

Some kinds of off-road vehicles are called **ATVs**. That means ''all terrain vehicles''—vehicles that can go where there are no roads. They can go over almost any kind of ground, or terrain, through sand, mud, and even water.

Some ATVs are hard-working automobiles. Forest rangers use them in the woods and mountains. Beach patrols use them along beaches. Prospectors use them in the desert. Ranchers use them for rounding up cattle.

Other ATVs are just for fun. Some are low to the ground with three wheels and big, fat tires. They look like large tricycles. The front wheel steers; the back wheels push; the brakes are on the handlebars. The gear shift is on the handlebars, too.

Another kind of ATV is called a dune buggy. It has special tires that let it drive across sand. Fishermen use dune buggies to go from one fishing place to another, along a beach, but in many places dune buggies aren't allowed any more. If they tear up the grasses that hold the sand, a beach can wash away.

Six-wheeled ATVs can go through sand and mud and even into the water like boats. They have boat-shaped bodies. In the water, the wheels become paddle wheels, pushing the car-boat through the water.

Wheeled ATVs will even go in snow if it's not too deep and soft. But if the snow is deep, a snowmobile is the vehicle you need. A snowmobile is not an ATV. It has skis instead of wheels and is built only for driving in the snow or across a frozen lake.

Many people think that there's a problem with snowmobiles and ATVs, though. Using them, it's easy to get into wild places where there are no roads. And that's bad news for the plants and animals in those places. Plants are destroyed, and the animals that depend on those plants die. And sometimes larger animals are hunted in places where they should be safe. Snowmobiles are loud, too. Once-peaceful wilderness is filled with noise pollution.

RACING CARS

Racing cars come in all shapes and sizes. Some look like airplanes without wings. Others look like rockets. Others look like diving boards or ice cream cones or jungle gyms on wheels.

Some racing cars are so small they can race inside a building. Some are so big and fast that the only track that is big enough is the one across the salt flats at Bonneville, Utah. Those super race cars don't race against each other; they race against time. They may go so fast that it takes them miles to stop.

There are all kinds of automobile races over all kinds of courses.

*The test cars of today are
likely to become the
family cars of the future.*

One of the most famous is the Indianapolis 500. It is held in the United States every Memorial Day, in Indianapolis, Indiana. The cars race 500 miles (805 km) around a track that was originally built as a testing place for standard production cars.

Grand Prix races are held on closed circuit tracks in Europe, Africa, and North and South America. These courses are especially designed for Grand Prix racing. Grand Prix racers are single-seat, mid-engine cars. (Indy 500 cars are like Grand Prix cars, but bigger.) One Grand Prix race, in Monte Carlo, is run through the streets of that city.

Road Rallies are another kind of race, for standard production touring cars. These are run in stages, along roads across the countryside. Scores for each stage are added up to decide the winner.

There are ATV races where there are no roads at all. The vehicles race up and down hills, through mud, sand, and water.

Drag racing is a popular sport, and there are drag strips in many communities in the United States. A drag strip is a flat, straight, quarter-mile (0.4-km) track. Many kinds of cars compete in drag races. Usually, though, the cars in each race are in the same *class*. That is, they are alike in speed or style or engine type. There are drag races for diesel truck cabs, midget cars, three-wheelers, stock cars, jet engine cars, and others that are just engines on wheels.

Stock car racing is popular in many places. Stock cars are general purpose, factory-built standard production cars. Stock car race tracks, complete with grandstands, are often a part of state or county fairgrounds.

An engine is the most important part of a racing car. Brakes are important, too. Drivers, along with their crews, are always working to improve their engines and make them faster. They work to make racing safer, too.

The people who design and build standard production cars learn a lot from racing cars. They use them to test new body shapes, engines, brakes, tires, materials, fuels, and safety devices. Many of the things we take for granted in our family cars began as ideas in racing cars.

(2)
HOW CARS WORK

The main parts of a car are the body and chassis, the engine and power train, the suspension system, the electrical system, and the brakes.

1. The **body** of the car is the car's shell, and when it is reinforced, provides the car's strength.

2. When the engine, wheels, brakes, springs, and steering system are put together, they are called the **chassis** (pronounced *SHAS-ee*). Sometimes the chassis and the body are combined into a single unit, called a **unitized body.** Sometimes the chassis is built onto a separate frame and the body is attached to it.

3. The **engine** supplies the power that turns the wheels.

4. The **power train** moves the power from the engine to the wheels.

5. The **suspension system** includes the wheels, steering, springs, and shock absorbers.

6. The **brakes** slow the car down or stop it.

7. The **electrical system** includes the battery, the lights, the starter, and the motors for the heater, horn, air-conditioner, windshield wipers, radio, and other electrical devices.

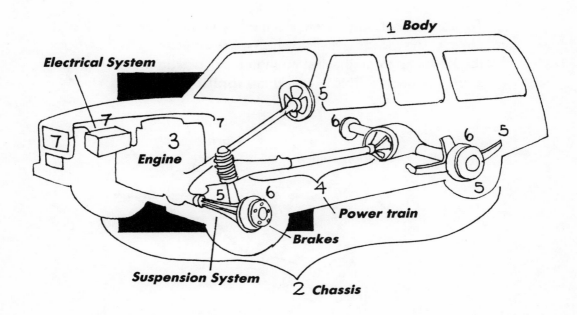

1 *Body*

Electrical System

7

7

7

3
Engine

5

6

6

5

4
Power train

5

5

6

5

Brakes

Suspension System

2 *Chassis*

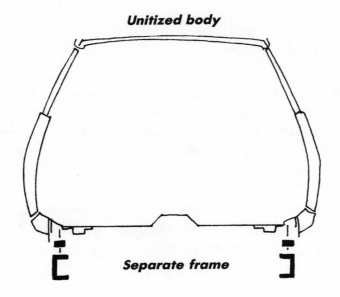

Unitized body

Separate frame

To start the car, the driver puts the key into the ignition lock and turns it. This closes a switch which allows electricity to flow from the **battery** through wires to the electrical starter motor, which starts the engine. This is called the **ignition** system.

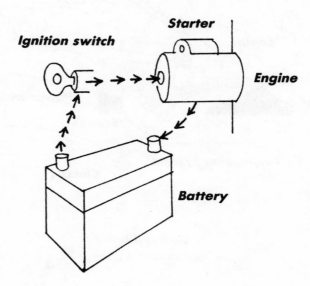

The battery stores electricity to start the car. It also supplies—when the engine is not running—current for the ignition system, the lights, the fan in the heater and the air-conditioner, the windshield wipers and defroster, the radio and the horn.

If electricity kept flowing out of the battery and never coming in, soon it would be all used up and the battery would be dead. So the battery is connected to the **alternator,** or **generator,** which makes (or *generates*) electric current. The alternator is turned by the power of the car's engine, once the engine starts running. The current made by the alternator enters the battery and continues to replace the current that is being used.

When the driver turns the ignition key, the current from the battery starts the electric starting motor, which turns the **crankshaft** in the engine.

The crankshaft begins to move the **pistons** and **rods.** If the car has a rotary engine, the crankshaft turns the **rotor.** (See page 35 for how these engines work.)

The **fuel pump** starts pumping fuel from the tank into the engine. Electric sparks light (or *ignite*) the fuel, which explodes and starts the engine.

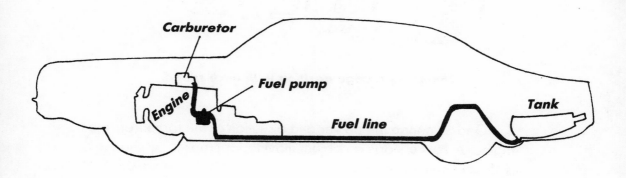

Once the engine starts, the electric starting motor shuts off. Now the engine is producing power, which has to move from the engine through the power train to the car's wheels.

The gears in the transmission start the work of carrying the power to the wheels. There are four or five sets of gears in the transmissions of most passenger cars, and even more in some sports cars and racing cars and in trucks.

(19)

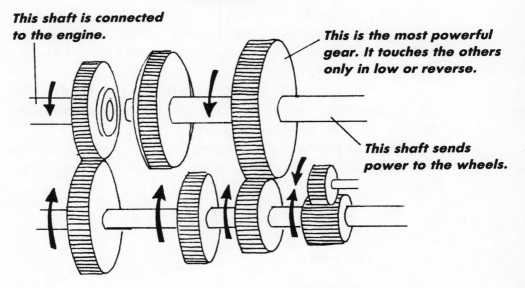

LOW GEAR

This shaft is connected to the engine.

This is the most powerful gear. It touches the others only in low or reverse.

This shaft sends power to the wheels.

The gears change position with each speed.

Gears change the power and direction of the force from the engine. A **force** starts an object moving, or stops it, or changes its direction in some way.

The gears in the transmission exchange speed for power or power for speed.

No matter how fast the engine is turning, it can't make the car go until engine power is moved to the wheels. That's the job of the gears. They control the movement of the engine power. The first set are the most powerful, slowest moving gears. (It takes a lot of force to start something moving.) First gear is also called low gear.

Then the second set of gears takes over. The car picks up speed. When it is moving easily, the gears are shifted again and the car is in third, or high, gear. Now it doesn't take much force to keep the car going. It's easy to change the speed by giving the engine more gas or less gas.

But if the car comes to a hill, it needs more engine force to move it up the hill against the force of gravity. So the gears shift down to exchange speed for that stronger force.

In some cars the transmission is automatic. This means that most of the gears shift by themselves as the car picks up speed or slows down. But even automatic transmissions have some gears that have to be shifted by hand.

The driver always has to shift by hand to make the car go backward, or in *reverse*. Reverse is powerful, like low gear. If the car is going up or down a very steep hill, it has to be shifted into lower gear by hand.

Some cars have an extra gear called **overdrive,** which helps the car use less fuel over long distances. To change to overdrive, the driver shifts that gear by hand, too.

If a car does not have automatic transmission, the driver has to step on a pedal called the **clutch** to disconnect the gears so they can be shifted by hand with a stick connected to the transmission.

The transmission changes a small amount of **torque** (pronounced *tork*), which is turning power, into a lot of torque, and sends it through the drive shaft to the drive wheels.

In a rear-wheel-drive car, the engine power is transferred to the rear wheels by a drive shaft. The drive shaft has joints, just as your arms and legs have. The joints let the shaft move up and down as the wheels go over bumps. Where the drive shaft meets

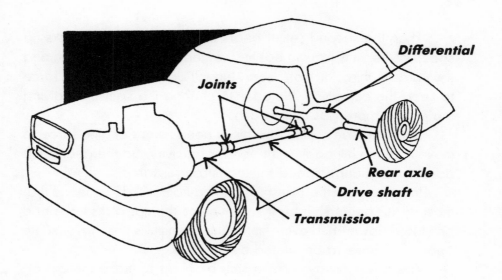

Differential

Joints

Rear axle

Drive shaft

Transmission

the rear axles, which are rods connecting the back wheels, there is another set of gears called the **differential**.

The gears in the differential do two things. They change the direction of the force from

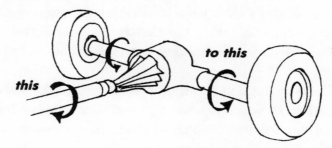

this

to this

And the gears let each wheel turn at its own speed when it is necessary. If the car is turning a corner, the outside wheel has to turn faster than the inside one. It has farther to go.

Many cars have **front-wheel drive.** With front-wheel drive, the engine power is connected to the front wheels by a **transaxle.** The transaxle does all the things that the drive shaft and differential do in a rear-wheel-drive car. The transaxle allows the front wheels to pull and steer the car at the same time.

Front-wheel drive makes better use of the car's inside space because it eliminates the big bump in the floor that rear-wheel-drive cars have. (The bump results from the latter's drive shaft, which is needed to carry engine power to the rear wheels.) And because most of the car's weight is over the drive wheels, front-wheel-drive cars have better traction.

Some cars have four-wheel drive. (See pages 10, 11.) The power can be connected to all the wheels.

The brakes stop the car. The foot brake and the parking brake are both connected to the wheels. Most cars have brakes on all four wheels, though the parking brake usually connects only to the rear wheels.

There are two kinds of brakes, **drum brakes** and **disk brakes.** Both use **friction,** the force that slows down moving objects.

Drum brakes stop the car by pushing a friction "shoe" hard against the rim of the wheel-drum to stop the wheel from turning.

Disk brakes apply friction against both sides of a flat disk that is attached to the turning axle. Many cars have both kinds of brakes.

Most brakes work by **hydraulic pressure,** which means the pressure of a fluid. Stepping on the foot brake forces liquid through the brake lines to press the brakes hard against the

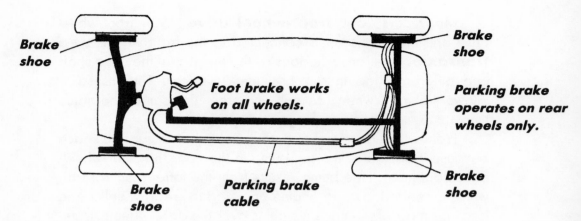

Brake shoe

Brake shoe

Foot brake works on all wheels.

Parking brake operates on rear wheels only.

Brake shoe

Parking brake cable

Brake shoe

wheels and stop them from turning. If the car has power brakes, stopping is even easier, because the brake fluid is pushed by power from the engine when you step on the brake pedal.

The parking brake is connected to the brakes on the wheels by a steel wire. It works mechanically as a separate brake system. Its main job is to prevent the car from rolling when it is parked.

(3)
HOW CAR ENGINES WORK

There are two main kinds of automobile engines, the **piston engine** and the **rotary engine.** Both are **internal-combustion engines,** which means that fuel is burned inside the engine.

In a piston engine, exploding fuel pushes the pistons up and down inside the **cylinders** and that up-and-down movement turns the shaft. Most cars on the road today have piston engines. **Diesel** engines are piston engines, too.

The size of a piston engine is measured by the volume of all its cylinders when the piston of each cylinder is all the way down.

In the metric system, which is being used more and more, the volume is given in liters. In the American system the volume is given in cubic inches.

Rotary engines work in a different way. In a rotary engine, burning fuel spins a rotor which turns the shaft. **Wankel engines** and **gas turbines** are rotary engines.

Both piston engines and rotary engines have: a fuel system, an ignition system, a lubricating system, and a cooling system.

(A system is a group of parts working together to do a special job.)

PISTON ENGINE

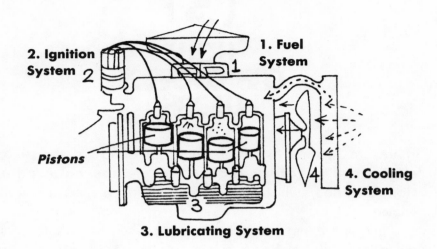

2. Ignition System   2

1   1. Fuel System

Pistons

4   4. Cooling System

3

3. Lubricating System

ROTARY ENGINE

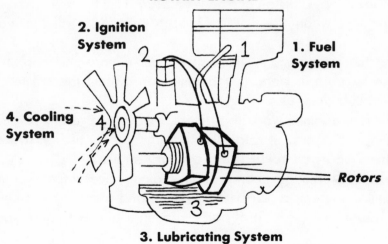

2. Ignition System   2

1   1. Fuel System

4. Cooling System   4

Rotors

3

3. Lubricating System

1. There are different kinds of fuel systems, but they all have a way of mixing air and fuel into a vapor which will explode and burn in the engine.

2. The ignition system takes current from the battery, strengthens it, and feeds it through the **distributor** to the **spark plugs** in a regular order. The spark plugs make the current into hot sparks which ignite the mixture of fuel and air.

3. The lubricating system pumps oil to all the moving parts of the engine so they will move smoothly and not get too hot. But even with the oil, the engine builds up a great deal of heat.

4. The cooling system moves heat out of the engine into the air around the car.

If the engine is cooled by a liquid, the cooling system moves the liquid through the engine and out to the car's radiator, where a fan blows air past the radiator to cool off the liquid.

LIQUID-COOLED ENGINE

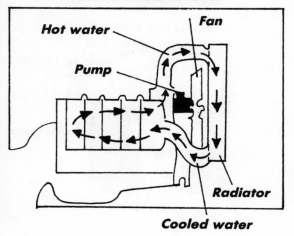

Hot water
Fan
Pump
Radiator
Cooled water

AIR-COOLED ENGINE

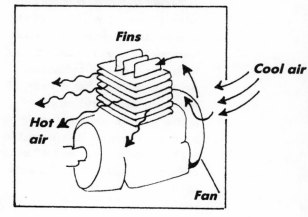

Fins
Cool air
Hot air
Fan

In some cars the fan is driven by a separate electric motor and only blows air past the radiator when the engine gets very hot or when the car isn't moving. However the cooling system works, the cooled liquid goes back to the engine to move more heat out.

If the engine is air-cooled, the heat moves out of the cylinders through fins in the engine wall. Fans and the movement of the car keep blowing the heat off the fins.

In all engines, the pressure of exploding fuel in the engine moves the pistons or the rotor, turning the crankshaft, which turns the gears, which turn the drive shaft, which turns the wheels, which move the car.

HOW A GASOLINE PISTON ENGINE WORKS

1. Fuel must be mixed with air in order to burn. It is mixed in the *carburetor*, to produce a vapor. This vapor is drawn through one-way holes called *valves*, to the top of the cylinders. An engine may have four, six, eight, or more cylinders. If the engine uses a *fuel injection* system, the fuel is injected into a chamber at the end of each cylinder where it mixes with the air to form a vapor.

CARBURETOR ENGINE

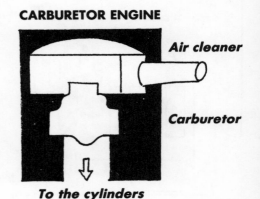

Air cleaner

Carburetor

To the cylinders

FUEL INJECTION ENGINE CYLINDER

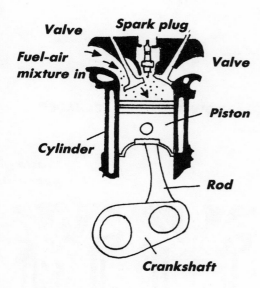

Valve

Spark plug

Fuel-air mixture in

Valve

Piston

Cylinder

Rod

Crankshaft

CARBURETOR ENGINE CYLINDER

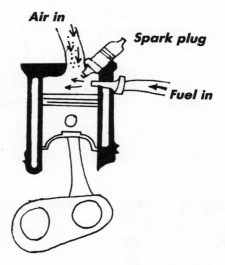

Air in

Spark plug

Fuel in

2. At the top of each cylinder there is a spark plug, getting current from the distributor. The tip of the spark plug has two stiff wires with a little space between them. When the current jumps across this space it makes a hot spark which sets fire to the gasoline vapor in the cylinder.

Spark plug

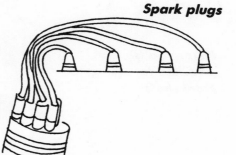

Spark plugs

Distributor

3. BANG! The vapor explodes, pushing the piston down. The piston is attached to a rod which is attached to the crankshaft.

INTAKE	COMPRESSION	POWER	EXHAUST

Gasoline vapor goes in

Spark plug

Waste gas goes out

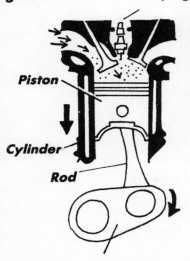

Piston

Cylinder

Rod

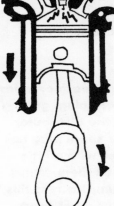

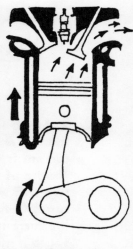

Piston rod is attached to crankshaft

The explosion in the cylinder pushes the piston down.

4. As the rods are pushed down one after the other, they push the crankshaft around just the way your foot (attached to your pushing leg) pushes the pedal of your bicycle around.

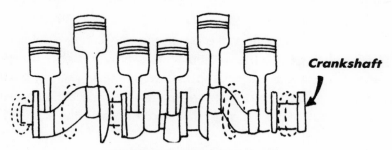

Crankshaft

The up-and-down strokes turn the crankshaft.

5. The crankshaft turns the gears in the transmission. The gears turn the drive shaft. The drive shaft turns the differential gears, which turn the wheels which move the car.

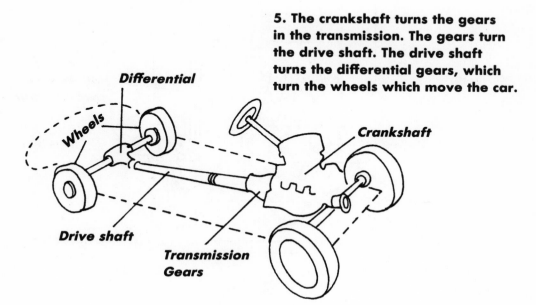

Differential

Wheels

Crankshaft

Drive shaft

Transmission Gears

HOW A
TURBOCHARGER
WORKS

One way to make an engine more powerful is to enlarge the cylinders. Another way is to add more cylinders. Both of these make the car less economical to run, because more or bigger cylinders use more fuel.

Another way to make an engine more powerful is to add a **turbocharger** to the engine. Very simply, a turbocharger is two wheels connected by a shaft. One of the wheels is a **turbine,** which is turned at a high speed by the heated exhaust gases coming out of the engine. The turbine spins the second wheel,

TURBOCHARGER

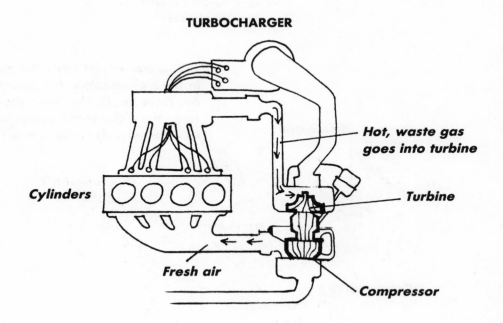

Hot, waste gas goes into turbine

Cylinders

Turbine

Fresh air

Compressor

which is called the compressor. The compressor pressurizes the fresh air that is going into the cylinders. (That means it squeezes the air molecules together.) Now the engine is getting more air, so it burns its fuel better. The more air, the more combustion.

A gasoline engine takes gasoline and air into the cylinder together and a spark plug ignites the mixture. But a diesel engine is different.

HOW A DIESEL ENGINE WORKS

A diesel engine doesn't have spark plugs. It has no carburetor, either. The engine takes in air and squeezes it in the cylinders until the air is very hot. The air gets so hot that when fuel is injected into that hot air, it ignites.

Diesel engines are more efficient than gasoline engines. That means that they deliver more power for the energy they use. But diesel engines are not as powerful as the same size gasoline engines. An engine's power is limited by the amount of air that can be burned in the engine.

In a gasoline engine there is plenty of time for the air to be mixed in during the intake and the compression strokes so the fuel can burn all the air the engine inhales. In an ordinary diesel, only 75 percent of the air can be burned because the fuel is injected directly into the combustion chamber. That's why more and more diesels are being turbocharged.

Diesels have disadvantages. They are hard to start in cold weather. Their acceleration is sluggish. They are noisier and smellier than gasoline engines.

1. **Air is drawn into the cylinders. The piston squeezes, or compresses, the air up to the top. Compressing the air makes it very hot.**

2. **At the same instant, a valve sprays diesel fuel into the top of the cylinder. Heat from the compressed air sets fire to the fuel.**

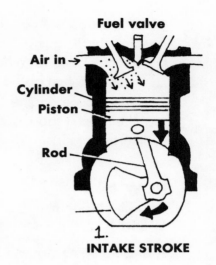

Fuel valve

Air in →

Cylinder

Piston

Rod

1.
INTAKE STROKE

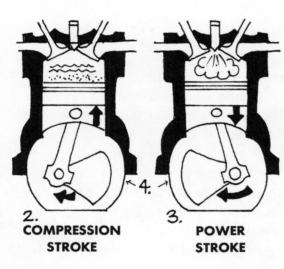

2.
COMPRESSION STROKE

3.
POWER STROKE

3. **The exploding fuel makes a lot of pressure, which pushes the piston down.**

4. **The up-and-down movement of the pistons turns the crankshaft, just as it does in a gasoline engine.**

5. **A valve at the top lets out the waste gas, and the cylinder takes in more air for the next stroke.**

5.
EXHAUST STROKE

HOW A
ROTARY ENGINE
WORKS

The Wankel Engine

The Wankel engine's design is much simpler than that of a piston engine, with fewer moving parts. It has a rotor, rotating in an oval chamber. When the engine is running, all its **cycles** are going on at the same time.

The Wankel engine is efficient, but it uses more fuel than a piston engine. It was named for its designer, Felix Wankel, a German scientist.

1. The fuel-air mixture is taken into the chamber.
2. The mixture is compressed and ignited by the spark plug.
3. The burning mixture expands and pushes the rotor around. This turns the crankshaft.
4. Burned gas is forced out through the exhaust.

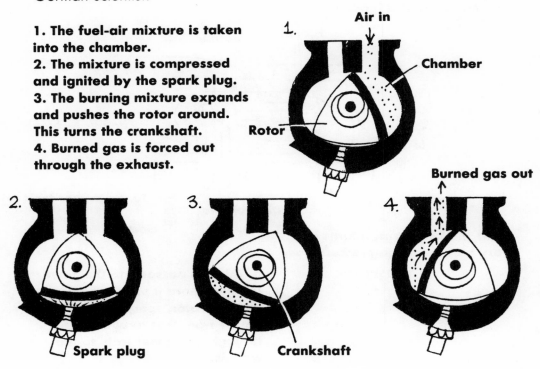

The Gas Turbine Engine

A gas turbine engine is another kind of rotary engine. It has two turbines, a gasifier and a power turbine.

A gas turbine has no pistons and no cooling system. It has only one-fifth the number of parts that a piston engine has, so it needs less maintenance. It uses cheaper fuel than gasoline.

1. In the gasifier, the turning rotor's blades spin and compress the air, throwing it into the burner, where it is ignited.

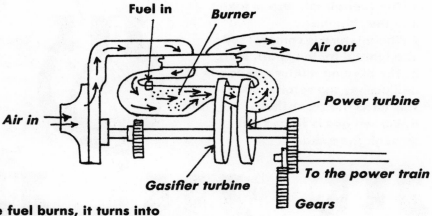

Fuel in

Burner

Air out

Air in

Power turbine

Gasifier turbine

To the power train

Gears

2. As the fuel burns, it turns into very hot, very high-pressure gas.

3. This gas passes into the power turbine where it pushes against another rotor, spinning it very fast. Power from that turbine passes through the power train to the wheels.

(36)

OTHER KINDS OF ENGINES

Gas and oil, **fossil fuels,** are becoming more and more expensive. Besides, they pollute the air as they burn. So automobile designers are experimenting with other kinds of engines that may someday replace gasoline and diesel engines.

Steam Engines

The earliest automobiles had steam engines. But they were complicated, sometimes scary, and often troublesome. Now inventors are experimenting with them again.

A steam engine is an **external-combustion engine.** This means that fuel is burned outside the engine.

1. Liquid is heated in a boiler, where it turns to steam. (The fuel used to heat the liquid can be kerosene or another cheap fuel.)

2. The very hot, high-pressure steam goes to the main drive engine where it spins rotors. That motion travels through the power train to the wheels.

3. The steam is cooled in a condenser on top of the car and returned to the boiler as liquid. There it is heated to steam again. The same liquid is used over and over.

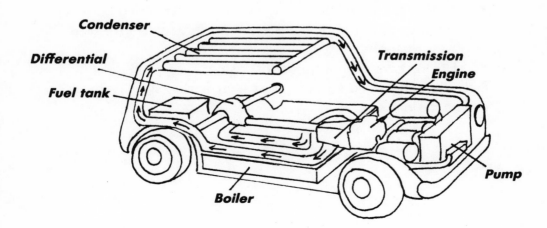

Condenser

Differential

Fuel tank

Transmission

Engine

Pump

Boiler

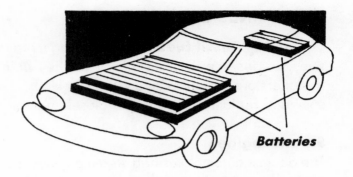

Batteries

Electric Motors

Some automobile engines run on electricity. Many early cars had electric motors.

Electric batteries supply the power to the motor, which turns and sends that motion through a drive shaft to the rear wheels. Electric cars were once the most popular kind of automobile.

The problem is that the batteries are very heavy, and they have to be recharged often—from every 20 to 50 miles (32 to 80 km) for a standard-sized car.

Manufacturers are experimenting with new kinds of longer-running batteries but these are very expensive. Besides, it takes a lot of energy to recharge them. If many people began using electric cars, there would have to be recharging stations all over. Probably, there would be arrangements for recharging automobile batteries at low-peak hours when power plants have plenty of power to spare.

Electric cars do not go as fast as cars using other kinds of fuels. But electric cars have no exhaust fumes, so they do not pollute the air.

Flywheel

Flywheels

A **flywheel** is a wheel that can be "charged" somewhat like an electric battery. It can be given energy by spinning it at high speed. Then that energy can be released to run machinery.

All cars have a small flywheel on the crankshaft, which stores up energy on the power stroke, then releases it during the other strokes. This keeps the crankshaft turning smoothly.

Engineers are experimenting with large, heavy flywheels that might power a whole car. But if a flywheel isn't constantly supplied with energy, the wheel slows down and stops. There are very big flywheels that power machines, but until someone finds a way to store enough energy in a flywheel that will fit into a car, it isn't a practical kind of engine.

The Stirling Engine

Some people say that the Stirling engine is the engine of the future, but it is one of the oldest engines we have. It was patented in 1816, in Scotland.

The Stirling engine can use a wide variety of gases as fuel, including hydrogen, which is plentiful everywhere on earth and in space. The engine works by rapidly heating and cooling the gas to make pressure in different parts of the engine. That pressure moves the pistons up and down. The Stirling engine is simple and efficient, but even after 150 years it is still experimental.

OTHER KINDS OF FUEL

Sometimes there seems to be plenty of gasoline for all the automobiles on the road. Sometimes gasoline is in short supply. Always, it is expensive. Scientists are working to develop other kinds of fuel for running automobiles—fuel that will not run out.

Methanol is a fuel like that. It can be made from plants, and plants keep growing. More plants can always be grown to make more methanol.

Methane is another renewable fuel. It is marsh gas. It can also be manufactured from animal wastes, such as manure. Propane, a part of natural gas, can also be produced from renewable sources.

Combining gasoline with renewable fuels is another way to conserve fossil fuel. Gasohol is a mixture of gasoline and alcohol, which is made from plants.

Some automobile manufacturers are already making cars that can run on alternate fuels. They seem to run well.

SMART CARS

Automobiles are becoming more and more complicated. So many things are happening at once in the engine and the power train that a driver couldn't possibly keep track of all the things that are going on. Some very new cars have built-in computers to monitor and regulate many of the car's functions. In some cars those computers process more than 300,000 instructions every second!

They control the timing of the spark plugs, the delivery of fuel to the engine, the automatic transmission, and the speed at which the engine idles. They monitor the engine, do rapid calculations, and put all the information on the dashboard of the car for the driver to see. Cars can have as many as fourteen instrument readouts on the dashboard, which are updated every sixty-five milliseconds. (A millisecond is 1/1,000 of a second.)

Some experimental new cars are smarter than some people when it comes to safety. Computers monitor many of the car's functions, and report what's going on—or not going on—by voice. The voice is a synthetic one that begins in an electronic chip. It produces the sounds we hear as speech, broadcasting them through one of the car's radio speakers.

If the radio is on, the computer turns down the radio and gives its warning through the voice synthesizer, repeating the message over and over until the driver takes action. The car might remind you to fasten your seat belt, or tell you that the door is ajar. At night, it would tell you to turn on your lights and remind you to turn them off when you park. It might also say:

You are driving too fast.
The gas tank is almost empty.
The door isn't shut.
The engine is getting very hot.
The oil pressure is too low.

(41)

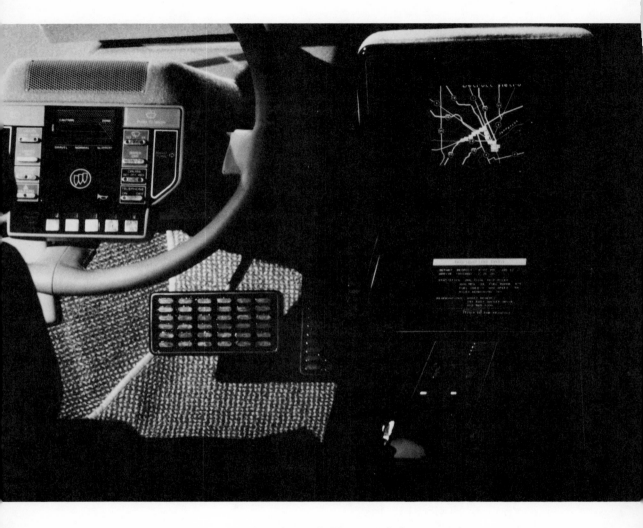

Among the many features of this smart car is a map navigation display (the upper screen). With a dot on the map, it shows the driver where he or she is.

Some smart cars now have photoelectric sensors on the rear-view mirror. If the glare of headlights from behind is too bright, the sensors switch the reflection off.

Smart cars will be able to listen and obey certain commands that have been programmed into their computers by the driver's voice. The driver could tell the car to put the windows up or down, or to change radio stations.

(4)
CARS AT
WORK

TAXIS AND BUSES

Most taxis are sedans. People usually call them "cabs." Taxi drivers call them "hacks," and call themselves "hackies."

Taxis are usually specially built. They have extra-large gas tanks so they have to fill up only once a day. They are heavier than family cars, particularly the doors and bumpers. Most cabs have two-way radios.

Hackies have to be very good drivers. They are supposed to know their way around the cities where they drive.

In crowded cities, where taxis make up a great part of the traffic, experts keep experimenting to find out what kind of cab is best. Some places use small cabs, which take up less room on crowded streets. These cabs carry only three passengers and the driver. Some places use larger cabs, like station wagons, which can carry more people going in the same direction.

In some cities around the world there are special taxis called jitneys. A jitney is a lot like a big, open station wagon with bench seats that go across the car or down the sides. Jitneys often run regular routes, picking up passengers and dropping them along the way.

*These three-wheel taxis are used
in the Philippines. They hold
two passengers plus the driver.*

Top: *modern buses are air-conditioned and have large windows*. Bottom: *this is a tandem-axle tractor pulling a trailer.*

Where many people regularly travel in the same direction, buses are convenient. Most towns, and all cities have bus lines. In some places the buses are double-deckers.

Many buses travel betwen cities. In places where there are few private cars, buses are almost the only means of travel. Farmers take their produce—even animals—to market by bus. Sometimes there are crates of animals on top of the bus and baskets of fruit and vegetables hanging out of the windows.

Some big, fast buses are built so that people can take long trips in them. These touring buses are very comfortable. The seats are up high so that you can see the countryside easily, and baggage is stored in a compartment at the bottom. Most cross-country buses have bathrooms, air conditioning, and observation domes made out of glass so that you can see the tops of mountains and the stars at night.

TRUCKS

Trucks are automobiles that carry goods from city to city, from door to door, wherever there is a road.

Trucks are built to do big jobs. Usually they have more gear shifts, bigger brakes, and often more wheels than ordinary cars. Most big trucks have diesel engines.

While most autos have just one body, trucks often have two or more parts that can be unhitched. The part with the engine, where the driver sits, is called the cab or **tractor.** When trucks are built, the cab is part of the chassis, together with the frame and all the parts that are attached to the frame—the engine, wheels, brakes, springs, and steering system. The section that carries the load is called the **trailer.** In some parts of the United

States, you may see two, or even three, trailers hitched one behind the other to a single cab. A cab with two trailers is called a double bottom. If there are three trailers it is a triple bottom.

Some trailers have a complete set of wheels. Others have only the rear wheels. The front end rests on the back end of the cab. These are called semitrailers.

Big trailer trucks look like railroad boxcars, and they do the same jobs. Sometimes whole trailers are loaded onto railroad flatcars. The containers of some trailers are lifted off the wheels and loaded onto ships.

Most delivery trucks are specially built for the work they do. Some are giant refrigerators. Frozen-food trucks are real freezers, meat trucks are not quite that cold, garden-produce trucks are just cool.

Bottled-goods trucks have racks outside.

Glass-delivery trucks have special outside racks, too, for carrying large sheets of glass.

Trucks that deliver hundreds of dresses and suits carry them on racks, so the clothes won't get wrinkled.

Trucks and vans that carry furniture are usually padded inside so things won't get scratched.

Trucks that take money from bank to bank are armor-plated. Instead of windows they have thick portholes for the guards inside to look through.

Trucks that have heavy things to deliver are built with elevator hoists at the back for lifting and lowering their loads.

A few trucks—those that do a lot of stopping and starting in one neighborhood—are powered by electric motors. Drivers call them "juice wagons," because "juice" is a slang word for electricity.

TANKS ON WHEELS

Some trucks are huge tanks on wheels. Most milk companies send their milk to the bottling plants in these tank trucks, which are specially lined with layers of glass, insulation, and steel, and are refrigerated to keep the milk fresh and sweet. Every night they are cleaned with steam and scrubbing brushes.

Liquid sugar for candy factories, and syrup for soft drinks travel by tank trucks, too. The sugar and syrup are usually pumped through big hoses from the truck to storage tanks in the cellar of the factory, or into and out of the hold of a tanker ship.

Oil for houses and factories, and gasoline for service stations and airliners are tank cargo. Tanks haul chemicals, liquid laundry bleach, vinegar, molasses, and even medicine.

Some street-cleaning trucks are tanks with sprayers underneath, for washing the pavements. Other tanks carry tar, spreading it evenly on roads through nozzles in the back.

The trucks that carry cement are combination tanks, mixers, and dump trucks. They carry all the stuff needed to make the cement and mix it on the way to the job. When the truck gets to where the cement is needed, it's all mixed and ready to be dumped into place.

HEAVY JOBS

Some trucks are designed to do big, heavy jobs. Each kind is built for its own particular work. They may have as many as ten speeds forward and three in reverse.

Some carry immense boulders or haul great logs.
Some move a whole house from place to place.

When a truck is carrying a really oversized load, an automobile with a big WIDE LOAD sign on it goes in front of the truck and another drives behind it, to warn other drivers.

A truck can also bring the parts of a prefabricated house in a single delivery. The walls have their windows already in, the roof is in sections, and the truck has everything else that is needed to put the house together—even the carpenters.

An automobile delivery trailer truck hauls new cars from the factory to the dealer. A ramp on the trailer lets down so that the cars can be driven off the trailer into the dealer's lot, where it can be cleaned and fixed up for showing and delivery.

Long, flat gooseneck trailers are often used to carry oversized loads. They carry tractors and steam shovels to places where they are going to work. They carry large tanks and boilers to be installed in factories or on ships. Sometimes tractors carry whole sections of a ship from the factory to a shipyard where they will be assembled.

Before sending one of these huge loads, an advance person drives over the route to see whether there are any low bridges or railroad underpasses, low electric wires, or sharp and narrow turns that the load will be unable to squeeze through. If there are, the router must try to find a road around the obstacle. If there is no other way, the router needs the help of the power company, the police, or the telephone company to remove the obstacle. When the truck finally starts out, the driver follows a map that shows exactly what streets and roads to take.

The trucks that carry nuclear waste must travel along designated routes, too. Those trucks, with their cargo in heavy lead containers, are not allowed to travel on some roads or bridges, in some tunnels and even through some cities.

SERVICE
ON WHEELS

Many of the services that used to exist only in buildings have taken to the road. This is especially helpful to people who live out in the country.

Vans carry most of the services. Vans have been turned into clinics for giving medical tests and "shots," coffee-break and hot-lunch wagons, beauty parlors, offices for keeping books and typing letters, traveling animal hospitals, and more. Vans are small laboratories, showrooms for salespeople, repair shops, and ambulances.

Bookmobiles serve people in places where regular library buildings are far apart. You can choose a book from shelves like those in any library. You have plenty of time to read your book before returning it the next time the bookmobile comes around.

Bigger trucks carry doctors, X-ray machines, and other medical equipment to factories, to very large farms and orchards at harvesttime, and to crowded areas where there are not enough hospitals. The doctors can examine a great number of people in a short time, where they live or work.

The United States Postal Service has highway post offices that carry mail, and people to sort and cancel it and do other post office business on the way.

Television control rooms on wheels can carry all the equipment needed for televising a program anywhere they happen to be. There are cameras and a control room, video-tape-recording equipment, a transmitter dish for relaying the picture to a studio or to a satellite, and even a generator to supply the power all that equipment needs.

Machine shops on wheels go to fix things that are too big or clumsy to bring to them. They go to farms to fix broken tractors or other farm machinery. They go to boatyards to fix boats. They have lathes and drills for making new parts and welding machinery for putting things back together again.

There are schools on wheels. Voter-registration booths on wheels carry polling booths, so that people who have never voted before can learn how to use them. In some places there are even churches on wheels.

TO THE RESCUE

Whenever you need help, it is fairly certain to arrive in some kind of automobile.

If you call the police, the officer at the desk will call the patrol car closest to your location on a two-way radio. Usually that car will get to you fast.

Big-city police departments have trucks that carry many kinds of emergency equipment—rescue gear, stanchions for blocking off traffic, police horses for crowd control. If there is a sudden, heavy storm, police trucks even deliver raincoats and boots to traffic officers on duty.

When an ambulance comes to the rescue, it rides on extra springs so the patient won't bounce, even if the road is rough. There is a wide back door with a ramp so a stretcher can be wheeled in and out. Inside, the ambulance is like a mini-hospital, with medical equipment for the ambulance attendants to use on the way. They also use their two-way radio to ask for instructions and to tell the hospital what will be needed when the ambulance arrives at the hospital.

This fire engine is a hook-and-ladder truck.

Fire engines come in all shapes and sizes. The chief's car is a sedan with a siren, flashing warning lights, and a two-way radio for calling in more fire-fighting equipment. The hook-and-ladder is a truck so long that a second driver has to operate the rear wheels. There are searchlight trucks, pumpers, hose trucks, emergency rescue trucks with all kinds of special equipment, and even a canteen truck to make hot coffee and sandwiches for the fire fighters.

(5)
DESIGNING AND BUILDING CARS

To build an automobile and keep it going takes many kinds of products from all over the world. It takes steel, aluminum, and other metals, rubber, glass, plastics, leather, cotton, porcelain, paint, gasoline, oil and grease, water, wool, chemicals, and much more.

In some countries, millions of jobs depend on automobiles. People design cars, build them, and fix them. They sell oil, gas, and tires, and build roads and bridges and keep them in repair. Other people work in industries that supply materials to make cars. And of course, many, many people drive cars, trucks, and buses for a living.

When a family buys a car or a camper, when a business buys a truck, when a city buys buses or fire engines, they all want to get the most for their money. So usually, they shop carefully and compare before they buy. That's why designers and inventors, engineers and other workers in the automobile industry never stop working on new ideas to make cars better-looking, and safer, easier, and more economical to drive.

They experiment with new engines and new power systems. They experiment with new shapes. If the outside of the car is designed correctly, there is less **drag**. Drag is air pushing

Top: *this test car was designed
to cut down on drag. Bottom: using
a computer to design a car.*

against the car to hold it back. If air slips past the car easily, the car uses less gas, is quieter, and handles better.

The design must also protect the passengers. Designers and engineers use life-sized dummies, jointed as people are, to test the car's safety under different conditions.

Designers also use those dummies to figure out new ways of using the space inside the car for more comfort and greater efficiency.

They try out new materials—in some cases, plastic or fiberglass instead of metal.

They work out better ways to build engines that use less fuel, even new kinds of fuel.

DESIGNING WITH COMPUTERS

Designing a car usually starts with drawings, after which a scale model is made out of clay. Then an electronic probe locates thousands of points on the surface of the model. These points are translated into numbers and programmed into a computer, where they are changed again, this time into an image on a computer screen. Using the computer image, the new car idea is checked and changed, and each change is programmed into the computer.

As each part is designed, the numbers in the computer mount up into the millions. Every collection of numbers represents a part of the car. The computer is programmed to draw the part on its display screen and to turn the drawing around to show that part from many different angles.

As the parts are designed and displayed, computers are

then programmed to make the parts shown on the screen move the way they would on the finished car. Gear shifts shift, window wipers wipe, brakes grab, to see if they work as they should. A computer can even test the strength of each part to see what it takes to bend or break it.

Computers don't design cars. People design cars. But computers can now take over and speed up many of the steps that are necessary between the designing of a car and its manufacture. Computers can also eliminate time-consuming or expensive steps. Once, designers had to make models, over and over, increasingly larger, all the way up to the full-sized models called **mock-ups**, which were styled and restyled. Full-sized drawings were made of every part. Models were made from these, which were corrected and changed. Then new drawings and new models were made until each part was just right. Now computers can take over all that in-between work.

A sample car is built and improved. New ideas are tested over and over before they go into production. It takes years before a new design finally reaches the automobile factory and the **assembly line**. When everybody is satisfied with the new designs, computers are programmed to tell the production machines how to make each part.

THE AUTOMOBILE FACTORY

An automobile factory is as big as a city. It has machine shops, upholstery shops, foundries, docks, restaurants, and bus and railway lines. Some plants even have blast furnaces and glass factories.

*Robots are used more and more
in automobile assembly plants.*

In one place only the engines are put together. As the cylinder block moves along, it is blasted, sanded, and polished. Holes are bored, sometimes from a dozen directions at once. Parts are fitted in and fastened.

In another place, a huge machine, four stories tall, shapes parts of the car body out of steel sheets. The parts move on to be welded together, painted, and upholstered.

Computers keep track of all the parts and schedule the production and the delivery of parts to the assembly line.

In some automobile factories, computer-controlled robots do almost all the work on the assembly lines. On other assembly lines, robots do some jobs and people do others. Robots usually paint and weld. Robot forklift trucks deliver parts to the places on the assembly line where they will be needed at exactly the right time.

Human workers on the assembly line are often called blue-collar workers. They call the robots **steel-collar workers**. Not too long ago the human workers on an assembly line were a lot like the steel-collar workers. All that was asked of them was to do a particular job at a particular time. Now that's changed. The human workers in an automobile factory add ideas and suggestions for better ways to make better cars. Robots can't do that.

If your family orders a new car, the codes for all the parts of that order are put into the computer, which brings them together on the assembly line just when they are needed—maybe a red body with a roof rack, white upholstery, a four-cylinder, turbocharged engine, air conditioning, and fancy wheels.

On the final assembly line, which is so long that you can't see one end from the other, all the parts are put together. At the end of the line the car is tested, then driven out of the factory on its way to you. How does it travel? Usually, on another car.

BUILDING YOUR OWN CAR

You don't have an assembly line, but you might have fun building your own car. It could be very fancy or as simple as a box on wheels.

Either way you will need: a frame, a body, wheels, and a way to steer. Your foot can be the brake.

Be sure to have your family mechanic check the car for safety before you drive. And drive safely!

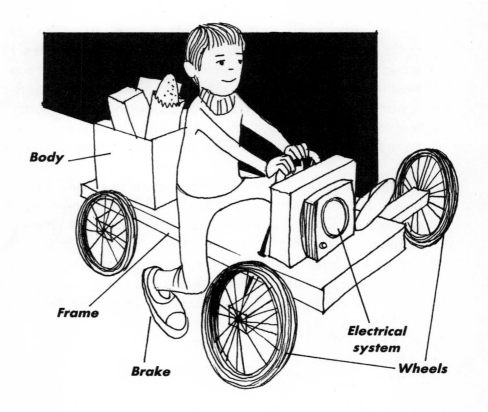

GLOSSARY

Alternator. A device that changes mechanical energy from the engine into electrical energy for the battery to store.

Assembly line. A line of machines, tools, robots, and people, along which an automobile is put together.

ATV. An ''all terrain vehicle'' that can go almost anywhere, even without roads.

Battery. A box for storing energy in chemical form, which can be changed into electricity.

Body. The part of the car that holds passengers.

Brakes. The devices that slow down the wheels of the car or completely stop them from turning.

Bucket seat. A seat shaped to hold one passenger.

Cab. The enclosed part of a truck that holds the driver and any passengers. Also, short form of *taxicab*.

Carburetor. A device in which fuel and air are mixed.

CB radio. ''Citizens' band radio,'' a small sending and receiving station that can fit into a vehicle.

Chassis. The combination of engine, brakes, wheels, springs, and steering system.

Clutch. The mechanism that connects or disconnects the gears in the transmission to or from the crankshaft.

Crankshaft. The rotating shaft in the engine which changes up-and-down motion to circular motion.

Customize. To change the interior or body of a standard car or van.

Cycle. Something that occurs repeatedly in a regular way.

Cylinder. The part of the engine in which a piston moves up and down. Most cars have four, six, or eight cylinders.

Diesel. A piston engine that runs on diesel fuel and has no spark plugs.

Differential. The gears in a drive axle that allow the wheels to turn at different speeds.

Disk brakes. Brakes that stop the wheels by pushing against disks attached to the turning axle.

Distributor. The part of the engine that distributes electric current to the spark plugs.

Drag. Air friction that holds a car back.

Drive shaft. The shaft that carries power from the transmission to the differential.

Drum brakes. Brakes that slow or stop the wheels by pushing against the wheel drums.

Electrical system. Includes the battery and all other electrical devices.

Energy. The ability to do work. Gasoline, oil, electricity, steam, and muscles all have energy.

Engine. A machine that changes the energy of heat to motion.

External-combustion engine. An engine that burns the fuel outside the engine itself.

Flywheel. A wheel that is given energy by spinning it at high speed.

Force. Anything that starts an object moving, stops it, or changes its speed or direction.

Fossil fuel. Fuel formed over millions of years from once-living things buried in the earth. Gas and oil are fossil fuels.

Four-wheel drive. Engine power transmitted to all four wheels of a car.

Friction. The force that slows down moving objects.

Front-wheel drive. Engine power transmitted to the front wheels only.

Fuel injection. The spraying ot liquid gasoline into the cylinders, where it mixes with air to form a vapor that burns.

Fuel pump. The device that moves fuel from the tank into the engine.

Gas turbine. An engine in which burning gases spin a turbine.

Gears. Mechanical devices that change the speed, power, or direction of a force.

Generator. A device that changes mechanical energy to electrical energy.

Hydraulic pressure. The pressure of a fluid.

Ignition. The spark that starts fuel burning in the engine.

Internal-combustion engine. An engine that burns the fuel inside the engine itself.

Mock-up. A full-sized model of a car design.

Overdrive. An extra gear that saves fuel over long distances.

Piston. A round metal canister that moves up and down in a cylinder.

Piston engine. An engine in which exploding fuel pushes pistons up and down.

Power train. All the parts of a car through which power moves from the engine to the wheels.

Rod. The stick that connects the piston to the crankshaft.

Rotary engine. An engine in which burning fuel spins a rotor which turns the shaft.

Rotor. A turning, or revolving, part of a machine.

RV. "Recreational vehicle"— a vehicle used for fun.

Spark plug. A device that changes electric current into sparks which set fire to the gasoline vapor in the engine.

Standard production car. A car built on the assembly line.

Steel-collar worker. A robot.

Stick shift. A stick connected to the transmission, for shifting gears by hand.

Suspension system. Includes the wheels, steering, springs, and shock absorbers.

Torque. Turning power.

Tractor. The engine and cab of a big truck.

Trailer. The part of a truck that carries the cargo, if it has a full set of wheels. If the front rests on the tractor, it is called a semitrailer.

Transaxle. Distributes the engine power to the front wheels.

Transmission. The gears that change the force of the engine into the power the car needs at a particular time.

Turbine. A rotary engine that changes the energy of a moving stream of gas, steam, or water into mechanical energy.

Turbocharger. Increases engine power by adding air.

Unitized body. Body and chassis combined into single unit.

Valve. A device for controlling the flow of any material through a passage.

Wankel engine. One kind of rotary engine.

INDEX

J 629.2 B 1984
Bendick, Jeanne.
Automobiles   Rev. ed. --
$8.90

47942

S-10/10   LU6/06   4circs   5libs

Hiram Halle Memorial Library
Pound Ridge, New York
10576